September 1996

To Beth and Bob Shea,

With appreciation for your love of Callaway Gardens. Thanks for your support. Come back soon.

Bo Callaway

CALLAWAY GARDENS

CALLAWAY GARDENS
Legacy of a Dream

Preface by Lady Bird Johnson
Text by Steve Bender
Photographs by Langdon Clay

CALLAWAY GARDENS
IN ASSOCIATION WITH
CALLAWAY EDITIONS

TABLE OF CONTENTS

Laurel Springs Trail

John A. Sibley
Horticultural Center

Ida Cason Callaway
Memorial Chapel

Bike Trail

Bike Trail

Scenic Drive

Wildflower
Trail

Pioneer Log
Cabin

MOUNTAIN CREEK LAKE

Holly Trail

Mountain Creek
Lake Trail

Gardens Country Store
and Country Kitchen

Rhododendron
Trail

Scenic Drive

Scenic
Drive

Fly-Fishing
Pro Shop

Gardens and Veranda
Restaurants

Bike Trail

Azalea Trail

Information Center

W

S

N

E

Callaway Gardens Inn

0   1/8   1/4

1.65" = 1/4 mile

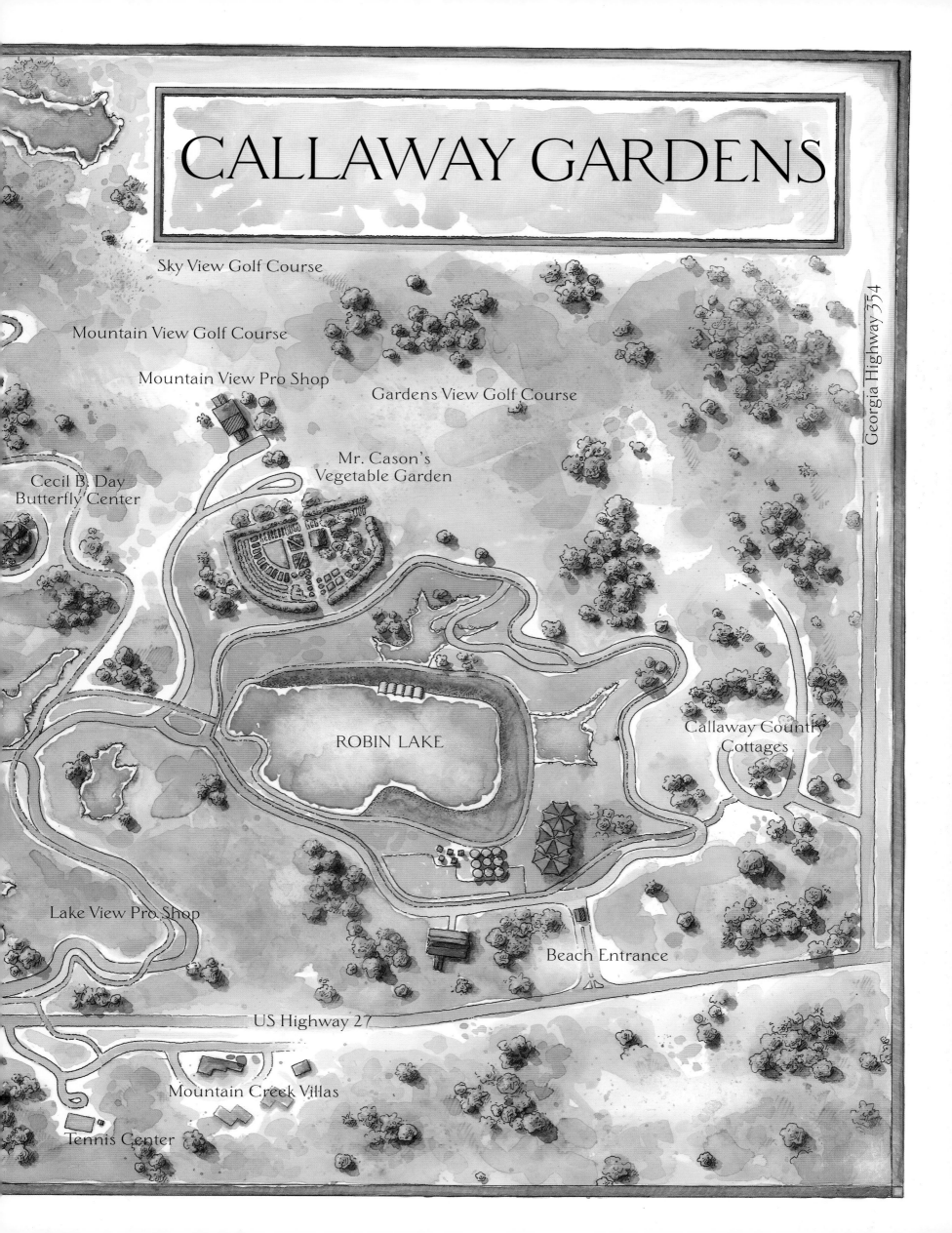

CALLAWAY GARDENS

Sky View Golf Course

Mountain View Golf Course

Mountain View Pro Shop

Gardens View Golf Course

Georgia Highway 354

Mr. Cason's
Vegetable Garden

Cecil B. Day
Butterfly Center

Callaway Country
Cottages

ROBIN LAKE

Lake View Pro Shop

Beach Entrance

US Highway 27

Mountain Creek Villas

Tennis Center

Callaway Gardens' Scenic Drive encircles the 175-acre Mountain Creek Lake.

9

Preface

In 1925, when President Franklin D. Roosevelt purchased the Warm Springs properties in Georgia, all to be dedicated in perpetuity to nonprofit, noncommercial organizations providing therapy for polio victims, Cason Callaway, living just 30 miles away, became intrigued. Meeting as neighbors, the two men took an immediate liking to each other, and visited whenever President Roosevelt came to Georgia, often as Cason and Virginia Callaway's overnight guest.

In 1967, during our White House years, Lyndon and I hosted a reception in honor of the unveiling of President Roosevelt's official portrait. Many of President Roosevelt's family, friends, and fellow workers were invited, Virginia Callaway among them. This was my first meeting with Virginia.

It was our common interest in beautification and the environment that brought Virginia and me together as friends. For my part, I think we, too, took an immediate liking to each other. And we often visited back and forth over the years between Georgia and the LBJ Ranch in Stonewall, Texas.

As a prominent member of the Garden Club of Georgia, Virginia was interested in highway beautification – using the rights-of-way of highways to spread native wildflowers – a subject that was one of my life's interests. The two of us were simpatico, especially on the subject of wildflowers. I grew up in East Texas, and exploring the pine forests was my favorite pastime as a child. One time, in July 1977, Virginia invited me to wander the woods of Callaway Gardens with her. During our walk,

PRECEDING PAGES: *Many of the evergreen, cultivated azaleas along Callaway Gardens' lakeshores are descendants of Asian species collected in the Himalayas in the 19th century. Others are the result of intensive hybridizing (or crossbreeding) programs by breeders in this country. The technique of hybridizing azaleas is relatively simple. The pollen is transferred from the anther of one parent to the stigma of the other parent. The flower is then protected from contamination by other pollen. Later, the seeds are gathered and made ready for planting.*

we came upon a vibrant orange, late-blooming prunifolia azalea. It is endemic to that area, and these flowers grew wild along a creek in a blaze of color. I especially recall how she walked faster and farther than I could, even though I was fairly young!

Among my earliest memories of Virginia are those of her great energy and drive combined with a genteel charm. She was the epitome of a Southern lady, but that's not to say she lacked steel or strength. Her resolve, sensitivity, and can-do spirit, along with those of her husband, Cason, are clearly evident in the words and pictures on these pages. Early on, it became clear to me that these two had an enduring love affair with the land. One of the regrets of this long lifetime of mine was that I didn't know her husband. Together, they left their imprimatur on the land and the lives of countless people.

Cason and Virginia Callaway with their dog, Rex Muddynose, July 4, 1937.

What began for Cason and Virginia as a picnic at Blue Springs, and an alluring idea for a weekend retreat for their family, took on a life of its own. Fueled by their vision, vigor, and daring, they shaped the landscape with the eyes of an artist combined with the pragmatism of wise ecological and solid land-management practices. The Callaways had deep within their thinking the belief that the land should be used for the benefit of mankind. They believed that beauty belongs in the lives of all of us. What could have evolved into an enclave for the affluent turned into a haven for the public.

Callaway Gardens is a place where families can enjoy the companionship of nature. Swimming, golf, biking, hiking, fishing, and boating – whatever delights the heart – await all visitors. Supervised activities for children give their parents time to enjoy themselves on their own. One of the most imaginative additions to the summer fare is the Florida State University "Flying High" Circus. Student trapeze artists entertain the young and young-at-heart. I remember watching the children – and the circus – with utter delight.

But quieter pursuits also abound. What lovelier setting could there be for meditation or attuning oneself with the natural world? Here one can listen to the silence and feel its grace notes lift the soul.

Cason and Virginia knew the Gardens would forever be a work in progress. Once, in an interview, Cason expressed his hope that his grandchildren and great grandchildren would be "working on it a hundred years from now, making it prettier and more perfect every year." It fills me with pleasure to see their family firmly rooted here. They have made Virginia and Cason's highest hopes soar.

One of my happiest memories is of when Virginia was honored in 1980 with the first prestigious Heritage Conservation and Recreation Service Achievement Award given by the Department of the Interior. I was in the audience applauding more enthusiastically than anyone!

Cason and Virginia would have been proud of this stunning book. You will discover their presence on each and every page in this celebration of their lives and love for humanity. In summing it up, I can't help but think of it as poetry for the senses! . . . *a tunnel of mountain*

*Butterflies like this clipper (*Parthenos sylvia) *are attracted to flowers by their color; the brighter and more colorful the flower, the more attractive it is to a butterfly.*

*laurel leading to a secret enchanted place . . .
butterflies dancing on wings of angels . . . wild
azaleas in contrast against the forest's green
cloak . . . a stand of wildflowers spreading the
welcome of spring . . . the solitude of the chapel
whispering its solace . . . lace tracings of ferns
. . . trees trumpeting the coming of fall . . . fresh
vegetables "waiting to be picked" . . . the drama
of shadow and light . . . shimmering lakes mir-
roring heaven's blessings. . . .* Joy awaits the
reader! Scenes like this make me feel more
alive when I experience them in person. As
I wander through the Gardens, I can picture
the Callaways at work and feel a deep kinship
with them.

The words on a plaque in my own garden
make my step lighter each time I see them:

> *The kiss of the sun in the morning,*
> *The song of a bird for mirth,*
> *I feel closer to God in the garden*
> *Than anywhere else on earth.*

Brilliant dahlias (D. pinnata) *reach their
peak bloom in the late summer and early
autumn months.*

This is "psychic income" and best expresses my feelings about nature's splendor and the
satisfaction of working in the environmental
vineyard. Cason and Virginia would have
known intimately the meaning of those words.
They found, as I have, profound joy in the
sweet mysteries of this living earth.

Lady Bird Johnson

December 1995

"If you get simple beauty and nought else,
You get about the best thing God invents."
– Robert Browning –

Introduction

Just past noon on an early spring day finds me meandering down a wooded path beside a glassy pond. The water smells musky and fertile at its edge, as the last of the autumn leaves are converted into building blocks for life soon to come. Across the pond, azalea blossoms paint the water red and pink with their reflection.

The air is perfectly still. I feel I could rustle the needles of a pine 20 yards away simply by wiggling a finger. I hear nothing beyond the nervous chittering of insects and the complaining caw of a distant crow. I am completely alone. But I am far from lonely.

Then it begins to rain, gently, almost apologetically. Gnat-sized drops pit and shimmer the water's surface, making a sound like bacon spitting and sizzling in a cast-iron pan. For a minute — or is it five? — I am spellbound, held fast by the soft intensity of nature undisturbed. Finally, a wood duck whistles and pushes off from shore, sending V-shaped wakes across the pond. Lunchtime, I guess. It is time for me to move on, too.

But the trip home takes minutes, not hours or days. For I'm not wandering in a vast wilderness but trodding one of the many foot trails that crisscross and delineate Callaway Gardens in Pine Mountain, Georgia.

PRECEDING PAGES: *Rhododendrons are planted with azaleas to extend the blooming season along the Azalea Trail. In Latin,* rhododendron *means "rose tree." One way to tell the difference between azalea blossoms and rhododendron blossoms is to count the number of stamens. Azaleas typically have five stamens whereas rhododendrons have ten or more.*

In Christianity, the dogwood (Cornus florida) *bloom is a symbol of the crucifixion. The white bracts form the shape of the cross; the green spiky center, which is actually a cluster of flowers, represents the crown of thorns; and the reddish brown spots of color at the tips of the petals represent the blood-stained holes in the hands and feet of Jesus Christ. Native Americans once used the arrival of the dogwood bloom as a signal to plant their crops.*

Callaway Gardens is famed for a great many things, among them the Sibley Horticultural Center, the Day Butterfly Center, the incredible Azalea Trail, and Mr. Cason's Vegetable Garden. But to me, the Gardens' greatest gift is this — that in the middle of a world-class resort, teeming with tourists from every state in the land and from all over the world, I can walk 50 yards down any trail and feel completely alone with my thoughts. Here I see virgin woods, pristine brooks, and indigenous plants as they were meant to be.

It is a sight many visitors, in their quest for the obvious, never see. So come with me — let's take a stroll through this place called Callaway Gardens. All you need are comfortable walking shoes or a bike, and I promise I won't ask for tips.

The trees along the Pine Mountain Ridge were once predominantly longleaf pine (Pinus palustris). *Over the years, the pine has been succeeded by a hardwood forest, which provides magnificent fall color. Today, Callaway Gardens is currently replanting the longleaf pine on the Ridge.*

FOLLOWING PAGES: *Colorful cosmos* (C. sulphureus *'Bright Lights') brightens Mr. Cason's Vegetable Garden in the summer and fall months.*

This perfectly smooth lake, illuminated by a clear, brilliant autumn sun, mirrors a peaceful spot on the Wildflower Trail.

The Tour Begins

Wherever I've traveled, at home or abroad, I've found that the best way to get to know a place — to really know it — is by choosing the mode of transportation that takes the longest time. Driving is better than flying; biking is better than driving. Thus, Callaway Gardens' Discovery Bicycle Trail, opened in 1987, represents a stroke of genius. It gets you out of the car and introduces you into a cherished ecosystem in which humans, plants, and animals are equal partners.

The 7.5-mile trail features only a few gentle hills, so it won't feel like the Tour de France. The steepest downhill speeds you along at upwards of about eight miles per hour. But such a languid pace is exactly the point. Securely saddled atop your couch-potato-friendly, one-speed rental steed, you cruise past mist-enshrouded lakes, over chuckling springs, through verdant woodlands, always within the heart of nature. The trail leads to all of the Gardens' most popular attractions. But should you decide to stop along the way and spy on a blue heron, go ahead. Or park your bike and explore one of Callaway's walking trails. Your efforts will be richly rewarded.

FOLLOWING PAGES: *A portion of the Azalea Trail is called the Azalea Bowl because of the natural bowl-like shape of that area. The walkways take guests through a lovely labyrinth of blooms.*

This native deciduous azalea, called the Piedmont azalea (Rhododendron canescens), boasts a wonderful fragrance and a dramatic blossom. The delicate petals and long stamens are quite different from its cultivated cousins, the evergreens, which feature larger clusters of flowers.

Undoubtedly, Callaway Gardens' biggest seasonal draw is its Azalea Trail, where thousands of azaleas in more than 700 varieties blanket the hillsides every spring. Ironically, although the Gardens dedicates itself to the celebration of native plants, most of the azaleas seen here are evergreen species from Japan.

Why? Because the public didn't associate the airy, deciduous, native azaleas with the "true" azaleas commonly planted around people's houses. "People were not accustomed to looking at native plants, which are so gentle, fragile, and not very splashy," explains Beth Callaway, wife of Howard "Bo" Callaway Sr., Chairman of the Board at the Gardens and son of Cason Callaway. "They'd drive through the Gardens and ask, 'Where are all the flowers?'"

So, with the help of Fred Galle, Callaway Gardens' Director of Horticulture from 1953 to 1983, Cason Callaway set out to create a spectacle of color to lure in visitors, while also assembling the South's finest collection of exotic species. Mr. Cason and Galle deliberately restricted these azaleas to areas near the Gardens' main entrance, reserving the rest of the property for native plants, including many species of native azaleas, which folks often call wild honeysuckle.

As their nickname implies, native azaleas can be deliciously fragrant in bloom, especially the Piedmont azalea *(Rhododendron canescens),* Florida azalea *(R. austrinum),* Alabama azalea *(R. alabamense),* and sweet azalea *(R. arboresens).* "Their fragrance is unbelievable," one of the Gardens' curators told me. "The first time I walked through the Gardens with all of them in bloom, my jaw literally dropped to the ground." You'll find 16 species of native azaleas sprinkled liberally through the woodlands and along most of the walking trails. They usually bloom before the evergreen types. Prepare to be astounded.

The Azalea Trail at Callaway Gardens was begun with deciduous azaleas, and later, a collection of cultivated evergreen azaleas was added. Most evergreen species originate in Japan, where hybridizing has been practiced for centuries. Continued hybridization of azaleas creates completely new cultivars. Many of them cannot even be classified as belonging to one species but possess several lines of ancestry.

FOLLOWING PAGES: *Lakeside plantings of these late-blooming hybrid azaleas are reflected in the water, providing twice the beauty.*

Traditional Easter flowers, such as these lilies (Lilium longiflorum), begonias (B. x semperflorens-cultorum 'Cherry Blossom'), and hydrangeas (H. macro-phylla 'Merrit Supreme'), make April a special time at the John A. Sibley Horticultural Center.

But don't spend all of your incredulity in one place. Save a good bit for your visit to the John A. Sibley Horticultural Center. From the day it opened in 1984, the Sibley Center has been a landmark of design, frequently copied but never duplicated. The magic of this 20,000–square-foot conservatory is threefold: It changes every day; its horticultural displays are absolutely beautiful 365 days a year; and it seamlessly meshes indoors and out through 26 folding glass doors. Though each of these doors stands 24 feet tall and weighs 1,600 pounds, they're so well balanced that even a child can open and close them.

I enjoy the Sibley Center for its lush, huge tropical trees and ferns and for its daz-zling seasonal displays of flowering bulbs, annuals, perennials, vines, and shrubs. There's always a touch of whimsy too, like pink-fla-mingo topiaries composed of dwarf English ivy and pink earthstar bromeliads.

The tropical conservatory, one of the earlier display greenhouses of Callaway Gardens, was incorporated into the design of the Sibley Center. During the fall, visitors are greeted with ribbons of colorful flowers and hanging baskets brimming with mums (Chrysanthemum sp.).

FOLLOWING PAGES: *The Sibley Center is designed to blend into the landscape.*

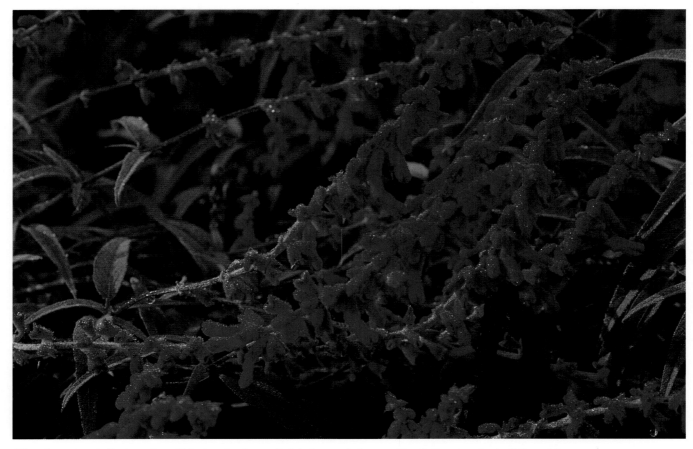

The velvety purple flower spikes of Mexican bush sage (Salvia leucantha) *spread in all directions in the fall sunshine.*

Then there's the ecological theme that runs like a freshwater stream through this and every part of Callaway Gardens. One day when I was at the Sibley Center, a staff member was pulling up bromeliads from a display bed and piling them into a wheelbarrow. "Surely, you're not going to throw away such beautiful plants?" asked an elderly lady standing nearby. Of course not, came the answer. The bromeliads would be composted, eventually providing nutrients for another generation of plants. Ashes to ashes. Bromeliads to compost. The natural system continues.

Adding plants like Mexican bush sage (Salvia leucantha) *and cosmos* (C. bipinnatus 'Pinky') *to a chrysanthemum* (Chrysanthemum x morifolium) *display gives the fall border a more informal, less rigid appearance.*

FOLLOWING PAGES: *Cymbidium orchids* (Cymbidium *spp.) are mixed with German primroses* (Primula obconica) *and daffodils* (Narcissus 'Ice Follies') *in this border at the Sibley Center.*

Hummingbirds are attracted to native evergreen honeysuckle (Lonicera sempervirens). It blooms from spring through fall.

The Greeks often presented foamflowers (Tiarella cordifolia) as tokens of affection. In Greek the name means "little tiara." The flower is so named because its tiny yellow pistils rise above the white petals like crowns.

The grass-like leaves of the spiderwort (Tradescantia virginiana) sometimes grow up to a foot long. Their resemblance to the spreading legs of a spider gave the plant its common name.

Several species of phlox grow wild across the United States, such as this blue phlox (Phlox sp.). Phlox leaves were once used to cure such ailments as nausea, eye pain, and skin disorders.

Although this flower boasts the name of atamasco lily (Zephyranthes atamasco), or rain lily, it is actually a member of the amaryllis family. Its common name comes from the fact that this flower usually blooms after a rainfall.

The vibrant red flowers of the red buckeye (Aesculus pavia) brighten up the shady surroundings on the Wildflower Trail.

The cymbidium orchid (Cymbidium spp.) is a member of the largest family of flowering plants with an estimated 15,000 to 35,000 species. Orchids can be found at the Sibley Center each spring.

The bottlebrush (Callistemon citrinus) *got its botanical name from the Greek word* kalli, *which means "beautiful," and the Latin word* stamen, *which means "thread." Bottlebrushes appear in springtime in the tropical conservatory at the Sibley Center.*

These wild irises, called yellow flag (I. pseudacorus), *are a refreshing touch on the banks of Mountain Creek Lake. Iris, whose name means "eye of heaven," was a goddess who delivered messages of love to earth, using a rainbow as a bridge.*

This cinnamon fern's (Osmunda cinnamomea) *fertile fronds are covered with the cinnamon-colored spores that give the plant its name. From late spring to early summer, this fern makes a handsome display.*

Daisy fleabane (Erigeron sp.) *was once thought to repel fleas and other unwanted insects, so early Americans dried them and stuffed them in mattresses. An old superstition says that a pregnant woman should plant a seed of fleabane. If the flowers are tinged with pink, the baby is a girl; if they're blue, it's a boy.*

The formidable thorns of the thistle (Cirsium sp.) *deter most animals from venturing beyond the first bite.*

Wild phlox (Phlox sp.) *in bloom is a reliable sign of spring in the South.*

The cymbidium orchids (Cymbidium spp.) *are usually at their peak during the Easter season display at the Sibley Center. The orchid family's surprisingly broad growing range extends from the polar regions to the tropics.*

The early morning sun burns away the mist to reveal this blue heron fishing for its first meal of the day.

The serenity of the Ida Cason Callaway Memorial Chapel provides an effective counterpoint to the incessant energy of the Sibley Center. Planned by Mr. Cason as a tribute to his mother, it is situated perfectly between a sparkling woodland waterfall and the banks of Falls Creek Lake. He worked on it for ten years, thinking all the while of the couples who would be married there and the children who would be christened. Unfortunately, he died shortly before it opened.

Built of native Hollis quartzite in the English Gothic style, the Chapel feels almost ancient. Its heavy wooden door creaks appropriately when you open it. Inside, the Chapel smells of long-unopened rooms. Six stained-glass windows depicting native vegetation and seasons of the year radiate color. But the building's premier feature is its powerful pipe organ, played every Sunday since April 12, 1962, by Julliard graduate Mildred Davis.

Mrs. Davis seemingly remembers every day that she has spent in the Chapel. She darts from memory to memory like a hummingbird among the impatiens. But her favorite recollection has to be of the day she pressed down on the pedals and discovered a large snake curled up in the organ.

Mr. Cason wanted the Ida Cason Callaway Memorial Chapel, named in honor of his mother, to be the heart of the Gardens, so he had this cherished place built near the center of the property.

Remaining calm, she motioned to a couple of visitors standing nearby listening to her play. Would one of them be so kind as to play the organ, or at least hold down a few keys, while she got somebody to remove the serpent? "But none of them even knew where middle C was," she says. Nevertheless, she managed to convince one young man to step into her place at the keyboard for a moment, and the snake was captured without disrupting the concert. "Ever since then, I've always thought that snakes love organ music," she declares.

A devout Baptist, Mrs. Davis has in her repertoire hundreds of hymns and songs, from the traditional to the contemporary. She often chats nonstop as she plays, as if her lips and hands belong to two different people. Mrs. Davis takes requests, but she prefers easy listening to rock-and-roll; she'd much rather you ask to hear "Precious Lord, Take My Hand" than "Good Golly, Miss Molly."

Pink dogwoods (Cornus florida 'Rubra') are found along the Azalea Trail and Scenic Drive. These lovely trees are generally cultivated varieties and are rarely seen in native woodlands.

Bright blue skies and rising mists signal the beginning of the fall season at Callaway Gardens.

Chinese holly (Ilex cornuta) *looks festive for the holidays with its bright red berries and a light frost around the edges of its dark green leaves.*

Paperwhite narcissus (N. tazetta) *have a wonderful fragrance and bloom from Christmas through January.*

Woodland patterns and textures, especially the silhouettes of trees and colors of bark, are more visible in winter.

Close to 30 percent of the butterflies living at the Cecil B. Day Butterfly Center are reared at Callaway Gardens in a specialized butterfly breeding facility. The other butterflies are reared on butterfly farms in Malaysia, the Philippines, and Central and South America. They are shipped to Callaway Gardens in the chrysalis stage by airmail.

When it comes to environmental education, Callaway Gardens has been taking the public's hand ever since it opened. Today, Callaway Gardens maintains an active, creative Education Department that, among other things, teaches the vital roles played by both plants and indigenous wildlife in our ecosystems.

But, as the saying goes, there's no use preaching to an empty church. "Women and garden clubs like pretty gardens, but to a large extent, men and children look at gardens and say, 'Boring,'" observes Bo Callaway. "You've got to take the 'boring' out of education." Well, there's no better example of making teaching fun than the Cecil B. Day Butterfly Center.

The first conservatory in this country devoted solely to butterflies, the Day Butterfly Center flutters year-round with more than 2,000 brilliantly colored butterflies. These splendid insects have no fear of people and calmly glide by as if you were one of them. Walking among them reminds me of diving in a coral reef among schools of curious, neon-colored fish.

On sunny mornings, the cold-blooded butterflies of the Day Butterfly Center can be found basking in the warmth of the sun to raise their body temperatures so they can fly. Thus, these solar-powered beauties are most active on sunny days.

PRECEDING PAGES: *The Victorian cupola crowning the Day Butterfly Center was saved from the 1890s home of Miss Virginia. During construction of the Butterfly Center, it was discovered that the cupola's brass door locks and hinges feature flower, hummingbird, and butterfly designs. The cupola must have been destined for the Day Butterfly Center.*

The scarlet macaw is the most visible of the tropical birds that share their home with the butterflies at the Day Butterfly Center. In addition to adding color and interest, the birds play an important role in controlling plant pests.

All of the Center's butterflies hail from the tropics, which might seem to betray Callaway's purpose of championing natives. But here it's necessary, because tropical species remain active year-round, while native species are seasonal. Still, plenty of indigenous butterflies frequent the salvia, lantana, and butterfly bushes in the gardens outside the conservatory each summer. During a five-minute stroll, I encountered tiger swallowtails, Gulf fritillaries, and clouds of sulphurs.

Before you leave the Butterfly Center, you'll learn all about the entire life cycle of the butterfly and even see it with your own eyes, from egg to caterpillar to chrysalis to adult. You'll walk among their favorite food and nectar plants and learn the role of these insects in the ecosystem. Luckiest of all are the visitors who can introduce children to the concept of natural beauty. "Every child should see something beautiful before the age of five," Mr. Cason used to say. Here children do. Later on, the effect will surely be profound.

The butterflies at the Day Butterfly Center are not the ones we typically find in our backyards. Instead, they are tropical species from the Philippines, Malaysia, French Guinea, Costa Rica, Colombia, and even Africa. However, some, like this zebra longwing (Heliconius charitonius), are found as far north as subtropical Florida. The gardens surrounding the Butterfly Center are designed to attract native species.

Butterflies use their proboscis, a slender straw-like tube, to drink nectar and other fluids, but they taste with their feet. Specialized sensory organs in their feet help them "taste" the right plants on which to lay their eggs. Tiny claws help them walk, climb, and roost.

Butterflies and moths belong to the same insect order, Lepidoptera, and are not always easy to distinguish. One way to tell the difference is the shape of their antennae. Butterflies have thread-like antennae with small knobs on the ends. Moths have tapered, feathered, or comb-like antennae.

The Southeast Asian demoleus swallowtail (Papilio demoleus) is one of 60 species of tropical butterflies that call the Day Butterfly Center home. Visitors can walk among 2,000 butterflies in free flight every day in this Garden of Eden under glass.

The cyndo passionvine butterflies (Heliconius cyndo) are the only butterflies known to feed on pollen as well as nectar. The yellow pollen can be seen still clinging to the proboscis coiled beneath this butterfly's head.

The Day Butterfly Center is designed to meet the environmental needs of its tropical inhabitants. A temperature of 84 degrees Fahrenheit and a humidity level of 74 percent provides ideal conditions.

FOLLOWING PAGES: *The butterfly garden at Mr. Cason's Vegetable Garden attracts butterflies with nectar sources that include the white butterfly bush* (Buddleia davidii 'White Profusion'), *orange Mexican sunflower* (Tithonia rotundifolia), *deep-rose native purple coneflower* (Echinacea purpurea), *and the lavender verbena* (V. canadensis).

The bounty from Mr. Cason's Vegetable Garden, such as these cucumbers, is used in Callaway Gardens restaurants and sold as "pick of the day" in the Vegetable Garden shop during the summer months.

Good ideas sprout like seedlings at Mr. Cason's Vegetable Garden. The last major project taken on by Mr. Cason, it teaches more lessons per square foot than any other garden I know.

Where else, for example, would you find black-leaved sweet potatoes used as edging for a flower bed? Or towering stalks of sugarcane employed as ornamental grasses? What other vegetable garden have you been to that features a stunning alley of blue-leaved spiral eucalyptus? Or a dwarf mint with leaves so small an ant might use them for throw rugs?

Mr. Cason wanted this garden to show the public how soil conservation and enrichment could dramatically increase yields. He also wanted it to feature the widest assortment of vegetables and fruits found in the Southeast. It does all of this and more. For example, it's designed in three semicircular terraces to avoid long, unbroken rows susceptible to erosion from water and wind. Prominent composting bins illustrate how to recycle garden waste easily. And during the dormant winter season, cover crops protect the soil. They'll add vital nutrients and organic matter when they're turned under before spring planting.

Probably the most fascinating aspect of this garden is the way it teaches us about our past, as well as our future. In addition to the latest All-America Selections of vegetables, it includes old Southern favorites such as Southern peas, butter beans, collards, turnip greens, and okra.

Early settlers made pumpkin pie by cutting off the top of the pumpkin, filling the cavity with apples, spices, and milk, replacing the top, and then baking the pumpkin and its contents whole.

When the foliage of muscadine grape (Vitis rotundifolia) *vines at Mr. Cason's Vegetable Garden begins to turn color, the big juicy grapes are almost ready to harvest for juice and preserves. Callaway Gardens is famous for its muscadine products such as preserves and sauce that are produced and packaged at the Callaway Gardens Preserve Plant. The recipes are adaptations of Miss Virginia's own favorites.*

There's also a section devoted to agronomic crops, which made the South what it is today. Here you'll find cotton, tobacco, soybeans, peanuts, and sugarcane. You might think this section appeals primarily to Northerners who have never seen a cotton field, but the staff tells me that Southerners enjoy it the most. Walking along these rows germinates fertile memories of youthful days spent in the country or on the family farm.

I'd be remiss if I left the Vegetable Garden without talking about fruit. True to Mr. Cason's wishes, the Garden introduces visitors to many varieties of apples, pears, peaches, plums, and cherries. It highlights unusual fruits as well, such as Japanese persimmons, kiwi, and jujube. But if I could steer you toward only one fruit, it would be the trellised rows of muscadines.

Black and bronze varieties of native muscadine grape (Vitis rotundifolia) *vines thrive on long trellises sited to catch as much sunlight as possible. The native muscadines were first cultivated in the South by Native Americans.*

The sunrise illuminates borders of orange marigolds (Tagetes patula 'Golden Gate'),
blue eucalyptus (E. cinerea), yellow zinnias (Z. elegans 'Yellow Zenith'), and green
mounds of morning glories (Ipomoea tricolor 'Heavenly Blue') growing on triangular
frames, also called teepees, in Mr. Cason's Vegetable Garden. In the background is a
spectacular bed of cosmos (C. sulphureus 'Bright Lights'). During the summer and fall
months, the cooler, morning hours are the best time to visit this garden.

Cason Callaway planted more than 600 blueberry bushes in his
early experiments. Agricultural experts of his day insisted that one of
these varieties, the New Jersey true-blue (Vaccinium sp.), could not
be grown in Georgia. Not only did Mr. Cason get it to thrive on the
Callaway farms but he beat northern growers to the New York mar-
ket by two weeks.

Muscadines, the best-adapted grapes for the South, have twined in and out of the Callaway story ever since Mr. Cason first started experimenting with them on his demonstration farm (predecessor to today's Vegetable Garden). Actually, it was Miss Virginia, the Gardens' self-taught horticulturist and matriarch, who really got things rolling when she substituted muscadines for plums in her mother's recipe for plum sauce. People liked Miss Virginia's muscadine sauce so much that Callaway Gardens eventually started bottling and selling it. Some folks recommend it as a condiment for chicken and wild game. But take it from me, its highest and most virtuous use is when it's generously ladled over vanilla ice cream.

Today, Callaway Gardens' restaurants serve all sorts of muscadine desserts made with grapes harvested from the Vegetable Garden. They include muscadine hull pie (Miss Virginia's own recipe), muscadine cheesecake, muscadine sundaes, and muscadine ice cream. My advice: Try them all in very large portions.

FOLLOWING PAGES: *Mr. Cason's Vegetable Garden features All-America Selections*
trial beds for flowers and vegetables. Here seed companies test different varieties for
their performance in the Southeastern region of the United States.

These bright red surprise lilies (Lycoris radiata) *shoot up from bulbs planted several inches deep. They are called surprise lilies because the bloom appears after their leaves have gone dormant. This exotic plant is also called the spider lily for its uncanny resemblance to a spider.*

Time for a Walk

The only drawback to consuming mass quantities of muscadine desserts is that your waistline eventually resembles the equator. Fortunately, Callaway Gardens' many nature trails provide the perfect venue for working off excess calories. Here you can inspect a plant collection, stand alone with your thoughts, and perhaps watch a kingfisher snatch dinner from a pond.

The Mountain Creek Trail, which starts down by the boathouse, ranks as one of Callaway Gardens' most spiritually uplifting walks. Coursing alongside Mountain Creek Lake, the trail passes beneath huge tulip poplars and loblolly pines, a living cathedral of limbs and leaves. Most lakeside trees wear scars near the base of their trunks, a sign that beavers have been hard at work. I feel sorry for the trees but can't help but admire the animals' tireless industry.

Early fall color brightens the Discovery Bicycle Trail.

A contemplative place and at the same time visually vibrant, the Holly Trail appeals to the pure horticulturist in me. More than 350 mature specimens of holly line the paths on either side of the road. Many are native, but numerous species of both English and Japanese holly comprise one of the world's largest and most comprehensive collections.

There's much more to this trail than holly, however. As I enter the pathway, my nose encounters the most delicious scent in the world — the soft, refreshing perfume of tea olive *(Osmanthus fragrans).* This shrub's handsome evergreen leaves hide its tiny white flowers. So come autumn and winter, you usually smell the heavenly scent of an olive in bloom long before you see it. If I were a wine expert, I'd describe the fragrance as "redolent of freshly sliced oranges and lemons with bright notes of ripe peaches and apricots."

Brisk autumn winds cover the forest floor with pine cones and needles mixed with the brightly colored leaves of native sweet gums (Liquidambar styraciflua), *tulip poplars* (Liriodendron tulipifera), *and maples* (Acer rubrum).

FOLLOWING PAGES: *The bald cypress* (Taxodium distichum) *was one of Miss Virginia's favorites. The knobby "knees" sprouting all around the base of the trunk appear when the tree grows in or near water. There is some debate as to whether these curious structures serve as added support or as a means for submerged roots to breathe.*

Heavy clusters of berries on this beautyberry (Callicarpa americana) *provide brilliant fall color and a source of food for birds.*

Farther up the trail brings all sorts of wonderful surprises, including the beautiful, cinnamon-colored, flaking bark of mountain stewartia *(Stewartia ovata);* the startling, bright blue berries of sapphireberry *(Symplocos paniculata);* and the lovely white blossoms of common tea *(Camellia sinensis),* a true camellia and the source of cultivated tea. I also discovered one of Callaway Gardens' signature plants: paperbush *(Edgeworthia papyrifera).* This deciduous shrub flaunts nodding, yellow flowers in the dead of winter and very early spring. I've seen it nowhere else.

The Laurel Springs Trail, one of Callaway Gardens' most secluded and intimate, is also among its most didactic. All along the way, interpretive signs tell the story behind the story. For example, sweet gum derives its botanical name, *Liquidambar,* from its sticky, golden sap, called "liquid amber," that was once used in chewing gum. In addition, sourwood gets its common name from the sour, oxalic acid in the leaves. Visitors also learn that beekeepers mercilessly chop down the trail's namesake, mountain laurel, because its pollen makes honey poisonous.

The fragrant yellow blossoms of leatherleaf mahonia (M. bealei) *bloom in February and give rise to dark blue berries in the summer.*

Fred Galle, former Director of Horticulture at Callaway Gardens, created stunning specimens from hybrid crosses of native azaleas.

The Wildflower Trail lives as a lasting tribute to Miss Virginia. More than anything else, she loved wildflowers. "Mother would go on three- and four-mile walks into the woods and get very involved with the flowers there," recalls Bo.

This trail begins with a stroll through lanky, swamp sunflowers that gild the air with their bright yellow blooms in autumn. Farther along one finds many of Miss Virginia's favorites — wild ginger, Indian pinks, ferns, and bog plants — tucked beneath tall hardwoods. As always, you encounter the unexpected. I thought Adam's needle *(Yucca filamentosa)* was a sun-loving desert plant, but this succulent grows happily here in the shade of tall hard-woods. Then there's the patch of primitive club moss *(Lycopodium flabelliforme),* which people traditionally gather for Christmas decorations and call "creeping cedar" or "ground pine." Club moss is very picky about where it grows. So admire it here, but let it be.

These flag irises (Iris sp.) thrive on the banks of Callaway Gardens' lakes.

Mountain laurel (Kalmia latifolia) grown in direct sunlight will flower more heavily than those grown in the shade of the forest.

FOLLOWING PAGES: *Azaleas bloom in a wide array of colors – white, pink, lavender, and red. Although beautiful to look at, the blooms of hybrid azaleas have no fragrance.*

This desolate cotton field is how Callaway Gardens looked in the 1930s. This photograph was taken where the Fly-Fishing Shop now stands, and looks across what is now Mountain Creek Lake.

Dawn of a Garden

You can't truly appreciate the monumental success of Callaway Gardens without learning of the humble land from which it sprouted. At the turn of the century, eroded, abandoned farmland, sucked dry of its nutrients by King Cotton, occupied much of southwest Georgia. Fortunately, a 17-mile-long bump of Hollis quartzite called Pine Mountain had escaped the desolation, for its rocky slopes and ridges defied the plow.

In 1928, so the story goes, Cason and Virginia Callaway picnicked on the mountain and discovered two things that would forever change their lives. The first was a pond called Blue Springs. Its pure, cobalt blue water surging up from the depths captivated the Callaways. The second was a rare, summer-flowering azalea, called the plumleaf azalea *(Rhododendron prunifolium),* which they chanced upon one day during a stroll through the forest. Found naturally only within a hundred-mile radius of Pine Mountain, its red-orange blossoms ignite the forest in July and August.

The plumleaf azalea (Rhododendron prunifolium) is native only within a hundred-mile radius of Callaway Gardens. Since it was the inspiration for the Gardens, this azalea, also known as the prunifolia azalea, is incorporated into the Callaway Gardens logo.

The Callaways saw in the simple beauty of the pond and flower the possibilities for a weekend retreat. In 1930, they purchased 2,500 acres of land that encompassed Blue Springs and its watershed. Before they were done acquiring property, Callaway Gardens would grow to more than 14,000 acres.

Mr. Cason made his fortune heading up the family's textile business. Nevertheless, he fulfilled a long-standing goal of his to retire early from business, doing so in 1938 at the age of 44. He decided it was time to devote his full energies to a task that captured both his imagination and heart: bettering the lot of the family farmer. He developed his demonstration farm, a place where the primary crop was ideas. He experimented with new varieties of blueberries, strawberries, and muscadines. He multiplied a flock of 20 turkey hens and two toms into 5,000 birds in three years. Most important, he showed Southerners during the Depression that by arresting erosion, renewing the soil, and raising their sights, they could turn a profit.

An early morning sighting of a red fox is a rare treat at Callaway Gardens.

Dogwood (Cornus florida) *trees often spread as wide as they are tall, and they can grow as tall as 30 feet.*

Miss Virginia won the Department of the Interior's prestigious Heritage Conservation and Recreation Service Achievement Award for the successful efforts in propagating the once-endangered plumleaf azalea (Rhododendron prunifolium).

An astute, impassioned businessman, Mr. Cason regarded turning a profit as a vital part of all business endeavors, and he took it even further than that: "It's a sin not to make a profit," he instructed his sons. "You'll go to hell if you don't make a profit." Fortunately for us, Mr. Cason doggedly kept all of his projects on sound financial footing, which is why we see Callaway Gardens in its glory today.

A heart attack in 1947 signaled the long, downward spiral of Mr. Cason's health, forcing him to slow down. Satisfied with the farm's accomplishments, he turned his attention to transforming the agricultural wasteland along Georgia Highway 27 into a magnificent garden his family and friends could enjoy.

As always, he did things in a big way. He built huge earthen dams to impound water for lakes at a time when conventional wisdom said such engineering feats were bound to fail. They didn't. The Gardens now contains 13 lakes. He constructed mile-long Robin Lake Beach with 32,000 tons of sand, which filled 531 railroad cars. The day the Beach opened in 1953, it was the largest man-made inland sand beach in the world. And he refused to accept the notion that his prized plumleaf azalea couldn't be propagated. He assigned the task to a man he called Prunifolia Brooks. Brooks didn't produce a dozen plants. No, he germinated and lined out more than 20,000.

The beautiful tree-lined fairways of Mr. Cason's original golf course were intended to provide golfers with inspiration and, if necessary, solace.

*The heady scent of the Southern magnolia (*M. grandiflora*) fills the Gardens in May and June, thanks to Mr. Cason's generous birthday gift to Miss Virginia. The enormous blooms open up to ten inches across.*

If anything was worth doing, it was worth doing extravagantly. One day, Miss Virginia asked her husband for a single Southern magnolia tree that she could eventually climb with her grandchildren. He returned with 5,000 seedlings. Now mature, many of these same magnolias freshen the air along the Gardens' drives each May and June with the sweet perfume from their waxy, white blossoms.

Mr. Cason originally envisioned his property as a pleasant country getaway for family and friends. "But," recalls his longtime secretary, Jane Williams, "he soon realized the gardens were too pretty to be shared with only a few people. That's when he decided it should be a garden the public could bring their families to and enjoy."

To help them do it, Mr. Cason presided over the construction of 175-acre Mountain Creek Lake, a nine-hole golf course, a hotel, a restaurant, and always, more plantings. In 1952, the Gardens opened as the Ida Cason Gardens, named in honor of his beloved mother. In 1955, the name was changed to Ida Cason Callaway Gardens, and then in 1961 to just Callaway Gardens. Following Mr. Cason's death, his son, Bo, took the helm. Bo's son, Bo Jr., is President.

*Red tulips (*Tulipa sp.*) burst out of a bed of 'Crown Gold' and 'Crown Blue' pansies (*Viola x wittrockiana*) in the outdoor borders of the Sibley Center.*

FOLLOWING PAGES: *The understory of a forest is the perfect environment for azaleas, which prefer high, filtered sunlight.*

From the back porch of Gardens Restaurant, guests can watch Canada geese tending their young.

Par for the Course

At first glance, there's not much that is natural about a golf course. Unspoiled countryside simply doesn't feature manicured fairways, sand traps, and perfect putting greens. Yet, Callaway Gardens' four courses are integral to the Gardens. Native trees and shrubs embrace each hole. Many of the 150-yard markers sport bluebird houses. Every round played conveys the subtle message that natural splendor is worth conserving.

"Dad once said, 'When someone misses a shot, instead of cussing I want them to look up and see something beautiful,'" notes Bo. Callaway's Mountain View Course is challenging enough to make many people miss. In fact, it has hosted several professional golf championships.

When people ask what my handicap is, my answer is usually that I can't play. I still have an opinion about golf courses, however, and I would have to say my favorite course is Lake View. Why? Because Lake View's fairways are so expansive and hacker-friendly, even I couldn't possibly hit a ball out-of-bounds. Lake View's fifth hole is also the site of my greatest golfing triumph. The tee for this famous par-three sits on an island in the middle of Mountain Creek Lake. You're supposed to hit an iron shot across the water approximately 150 yards to the hole. Normally, I allot at least seven balls for a shot like this. But my very first shot arched perfectly through the air, was apparently blessed by God on the way, and miraculously dropped two feet from the cup. Minutes later, after regaining consciousness, I sank the putt for my life's only birdie. And I thought to myself, "What a beautiful place." Mr. Cason would be happy.

The distinctive peeling bark of a sycamore (Platanus occidentalis) *reveals white patches.*

FOLLOWING PAGES: *This particular season the All-America Selections trial gardens feature red salvia* (S. coccinea *'Lady in Red'*), *pink salvia* (S. coccinea *'Cherry Blossom'*), *orange Mexican sunflower* (Tithonia rotundifolia) *(foreground), and orange cosmos* (C. sulphureus *'Bright Lights'*).

Native yellow flag iris (I. pseudacorus) *foliage arches gracefully over cloud reflections in Falls Creek Lake.*

Voices of the Dream

Every garden worth its compost does more than showcase beautiful plants. In its style and composition, it allows us to hear the voices of the people who created it. Callaway Gardens is very much worth its compost. Every vista, every walk, every lake, and every planting expresses how Cason and Virginia Callaway each viewed the world and envisioned their roles within it.

Miss Virginia was a sensitive, intuitive, self-taught gardener who derived particular joy from private moments spent immersed in plants. The elegance of a single flower or leaf impressed her just as much as the gaudiest display. "She loved every wildflower," says Robert Marvin, whose architectural firm helped design both the Sibley Horticultural Center and the Day Butterfly Center. "Her whole self-image was in her wildflower walks." Today, when you see foamflowers, trilliums, and mountain laurels blooming at Callaway, you see Miss Virginia in each and every blossom.

An azalea's ability to cross-pollinate so easily keeps it in a constant state of active evolution.

The bright red berries of the dogwood (Cornus florida) *will soon become winter food for songbirds.*

She was a teacher, too, and used the Gardens to imbue her children and grandchildren with the love and understanding of plants and nature. Her lessons were so easy to grasp, because she never lost her sense of childlike wonder and playfulness.

Beth Callaway remembers how Miss Virginia made use of the 5,000 magnolias Mr. Cason presented to her. "She taught people how to collect the seeds, how to scarify them, and how to plant them," she says. "Later, she taught her grandchildren how to climb the magnolias. I'll never forget one day looking up with horror into those trees. There was Bo's most dignified mother going limb by limb up into a magnolia with my five-year-old."

Miss Virginia's influence extended far beyond her immediate family and Callaway Gardens. "She was a very active woman," remarks Bo Jr. "The thing that impresses me most about Grandmother is, although she was great with her grandchildren, I've run across so many other people whose lives she touched. For example, when I lived in Houston, a neighbor two houses down found out I was related to her. Tears came to his eyes and he said, 'Oh, that wonderful woman! I met her in Venice, Italy, when she was collecting seeds for her garden. What an impressive lady.'"

Southern stands of mountain laurel (Kalmia latifolia) *prefer cooler spots near streams, like this shrub growing on the banks of Barnes Creek in the Cason J. Callaway Memorial Forest.*

Canada geese lay their eggs in indentations in the ground. During incubation, the goose will lie flat and motionless with her long neck outstretched. While the gander does not participate in incubation, he is always nearby ready to defend the nest and territory.

At heart, Virginia Callaway was as much an ecologist as a flower gardener. In the 1970s, when the state proposed running Interstate 185 through Pine Mountain, she led the successful charge against it, arguing that the road would threaten the area's unique ecosystem. And though she dearly loved individual plants, she recognized that preserving the native topography and habitat took precedence over planting ornamentals.

"When Mrs. Callaway brought me in to do the Gardens' master plan," Marvin recalls, "she sat me down and said, 'Robert, I'm not bringing you in for horticulture — as much as I love it — and I'm not bringing you in for plant displays — as much as I love plants. I'm bringing you in for art.' She said the environment is art, and you select plants to fit the art, rather than let plants dominate." Thanks to Miss Virginia, Callaway's art is thriving.

A water oak (Quercus nigra) *on the shore of Mountain Creek Lake shades one of the best picnicking spots in the Gardens.*

These sunflowers were grown from seeds found in a birdseed mix.

Though Miss Virginia and Mr. Cason shared a common mission, their approaches and sensibilities diverged dramatically. "Mother would never have built these gardens in a million, million years," Bo declares. "She loved flowers and would be happy with a few by a stream. But the visionary, the risk taker, the one so far ahead of his time, was Dad."

Tireless, demanding, and supremely confident, Mr. Cason had been turning dreams into reality all his life. He built a textile empire by making rags from cotton waste others dismissed as useless. His demonstration farm was the most productive and innovative farm anyone had ever seen come out of the desolate, played-out soil. And when unbelievers told him no one would come to a garden located in the middle of nowhere, 70 miles from Atlanta, Mr. Cason once again proved them wrong.

He did so by applying an uncanny knack for divining how major projects would turn out years before their completion. For instance, Jane Williams remembers how her husband went walking one day with Mr. Cason around the proposed boundaries for 175-acre Mountain Creek Lake. "He told my husband that the water would come up to here and stop right over there," she says. "Well, that lake took a year to fill. And when it was full, the shoreline was almost exactly the path they'd walked."

The showy snowball viburnum (V. macrocephalum) grows up to ten feet high, with flower clusters measuring three to eight inches in diameter. These plants have been popular in American home gardens since the 1800s.

The Indian pipe (Monotropa uniflora), *or peace pipe, is a flower that contains no chlorophyll so it wilts immediately upon exposure to direct sunlight. This waxy, white plant's common name comes from its resemblance to an upside-down pipe. Once the flower has been pollinated, it stands straight up and turns a pale pink.*

"Grandfather, I think, had a restless mind," suggests Bo Jr. "He loved figuring things out to see what would work. And it's amazing to see how well many of the things he did have stood the test of time. A good example of his foresight is Mountain Creek Lake. When he was building it, he said he didn't want to have a metal drain pipe to drain it, because he was told that pipes last only 200 to 300 years. He said, 'I want this lake to last a thousand years.'"

Mr. Cason was a man who thought in terms of millennia rather than decades and in thousands rather than dozens. Bo explains his father's passion by recalling the words of Daniel Burnham, the great architect of the late nineteenth century who designed Union Station in Washington, D.C.: "'Make no little plans — they have no capacity to stir men's blood. . . . Make big plans.' Well, that was Dad. He never made little plans. He always thought on a huge scale." Because of the height and depth of Mr. Cason's vision, Callaway Gardens stirs our hearts.

There are many springs and streams in the Pine Mountain area. On a winter day, ice forms from the spray of a waterfall in this stream.

FOLLOWING PAGES: *Foxgloves* (Digitalis purpurea 'Foxy') *point skyward in the Herb Garden along with snapdragons* (Antirrhinum majus), *pansies* (Viola x wittrockiana), *and poppies* (Papaver spp.).

PRECEDING PAGES: *Cason Callaway insisted that the Scenic Drive curve through the Gardens so that visitors would be pleasantly surprised by the lovely sights revealed around every bend, such as this view across a lake.*

The blossoms of mountain laurel (Kalmia latifolia) *may be white, pink, or rose. The stamens have a spring-like mechanism that shoots pollen into the air when tripped by bees or other pollinating insects, thereby ensuring cross-pollination.*

The Callaway Difference

Beautiful public gardens exist all across the land. Many feature quiet lakes, scenic trails, lush woodlands, and magnificent seasonal displays. What, then, sets Callaway Gardens apart?

The first is scale. Huge scale. Although the formal gardens cover little more than 2,500 acres, the entire property encompasses 14,000 acres. This makes it larger than the largest state park in Georgia. It's this awesome size that lets Callaway Gardens act as a buffer against commercial and residential development and as a refuge for indigenous plants and wildlife. And it's this very same size that allows you to find yourself in blissful isolation on one of the Gardens' many trails.

The scale of Callaway Gardens is evident in its plantings, too. Where another garden might display a hundred azaleas, Callaway presents 50,000. Where another garden might plant a thousand ornamental trees and shrubs, Callaway plants 300 times that number.

Azaleas in pastel shades add to the serenity of spring at Callaway Gardens. The leaves of the evergreen azaleas offer a variety of colors and textures as well.

Callaway's second hallmark is its dedication to native plants. The area around Pine Mountain comprises a unique melting pot for plants of both the Piedmont and Coastal Plain regions. Natural scientists speculate that as a prehistoric sea traveled up the riverbeds of the Flint and Chattahoochee rivers, it provided a migration route for coastal plants. At the same time, Pine Mountain's verdant woodlands and cool springs sheltered mountain plants.

But the key to this extraordinarily diverse ecosystem is the topography of Pine Mountain itself. Its angular terrain and rocky soil prevented land clearing for farms, thus preserving indigenous vegetation.

Today, representatives of both upland and lowland plants prosper throughout the Gardens. American beech *(Fagus grandifolia)*, mountain laurel *(Kalmia latifolia)*, wake robin *(Trillium flexipes)*, tulip poplar *(Liriodendron tulipifera)*, chestnut oak *(Quercus prinus)*, redbud *(Cercis canadensis)*, wild ginger *(Hexastylis* sp.*)*, and strawberry bush *(Euonymus americanus)* exemplify upland species. Bottlebrush buckeye *(Aesculus parviflora)*, longleaf pine *(Pinus palustris)*, dwarf palmetto *(Sabal minor)*, oakleaf hydrangea *(H. quercifolia)*, wax myrtle *(Myrica cerifera)*, sweet bay *(Magnolia virginiana)*, and plumleaf azalea *(Rhododendron prunifolium)* carry the banner for lowland plants.

A fallen branch is lodged in a fork of this tree at the Cason J. Callaway Memorial Forest. A tapestry of mosses and lichens adorn the tree's bark. Lichens are compound plants made up of algae and fungus; it is a symbiotic relationship in which each provides the other with essential nutrients.

After they die, trees in the Cason J. Callaway Memorial Forest are left undisturbed so that they can decompose and enrich the soil.

Callaway Gardens' third claim to fame is its year-round appeal. Visitors by the thousands throng to the Gardens each spring to be thrilled by breathtaking displays of azaleas, but to sum up Callaway's charm simply as "azaleas" is like tasting a delicious cake and announcing, "It's the ginger." Ginger may be a key ingredient, but if it weren't for the flour, sugar, shortening, eggs, and other spices, the ginger by itself would fall flat.

No, to really see and know Callaway, you must return every season. Come in spring for the wildflowers, azaleas, rhododendrons, and flowering trees. Come in summer for the flower borders, crape myrtles, and Vegetable Garden. Come in fall for the hollies, beautyberry, witch hazel, sasanquas, and all the native trees in their dazzling fall colors, and return to walk in winter woods, where the forest is silent and the afternoon sun softly illuminates the bark and branches of noble hardwoods.

Great egrets, members of the white heron family, are often found foraging for small fish and frogs in the shallow water along the edge of Mountain Creek Lake.

Azaleas along the shore add splashes of color to the lakeside trees.

The strong silken web of this orb weaver spider is almost complete. Educational discovery programs at Callaway Gardens present these and other often misunderstood creatures in a more positive light.

Continuing commitment to public education marks Callaway Gardens' fourth area of achievement. A talented, knowledgeable staff of horticulturists, naturalists, and volunteers teach schoolchildren and other visitors about the wonders of nature. Discovery programs explore such topics as "Butterflies and Blossoms," "Thyme for Herbs," "Vegetable Garden Ventures," and "Birdwatching Basics." Callaway Gardens' quarterly newsletter, *Inside the Gardens,* tells us why snakes and spiders aren't sinister, why bats belong, and why river otters should run wild.

I'd be negligent if I didn't mention some of the wonderful plants now in the nursery trade and available to the public because of the eagle-eyed staff at Callaway Gardens. In each case, a canny horticulturist spotted a new plant, discerned what was different about it and what made it valuable, and saved it for propagation.

Thanks to such insight, we now can enjoy *'Callaway'* wild ginger *(Hexastylis shuttleworthii 'Callaway'),* a lovely evergreen groundcover with mottled, silver-and-green foliage; 'Hummingbird' summersweet (*Clethra alnifolia* 'Hummingbird'), a dwarf form of this fragrant, summer-blooming shrub, discovered near Callaway Gardens' Hummingbird Lake; and *'Callaway'* crabapple (*Malus* 'Callaway'), probably the best crabapple for the South.

Lady Banks roses (Rosa banksia 'Alba') decorate the arbor leading into Victory Garden South where southern segments of the popular PBS gardening program, "The Victory Garden," have been shot since 1980.

118

Clay pots on the steps to the porch of Victory Garden South overflow with sweet alyssum (Lobularia maritima) and yellow daffodils (Narcissus spp.).

The huge, papery leaves and flexible stems of this big-leaf magnolia (M. macrophylla) reach for the filtered sunlight of a hardwood forest.

But the thing that most distinguishes Callaway Gardens is the fact that it exists today in what appears to be an almost primeval state. Remember back in the beginning, when I described a walk through virgin woods? Well, that's not exactly true. Most of Callaway's land had been clear-cut for farming back in the mid-1800s, then used to grow cotton, then abandoned. So, the magnificent woodlands we see today represent carefully nurtured second growth.

Bo dispels the notion that all his parents had to do was refine the natural grandeur already there. He says, "A few years before Dad died, he laughed and said to me, 'You know, someday somebody is going to say, Wasn't old man Callaway lucky to find such a beautiful place?' The irony is that in the beginning, nothing here was prettier than any other place and most of it was uglier."

To Bo Jr., the lesson of Callaway Gardens is that one committed individual pursuing a dream can make a huge difference. "I used to think the world was so vast, what impact can I have?" he says. "What Grandfather proved is that one person can have a tremendous impact. In the span of a hundred years, this land went from very little use to economic ruin to something that is truly beautiful. A hundred years — that's a blink in time. So the point is, what we do does matter."

FOLLOWING PAGES: *This lush, fern-lined portion of Barnes Creek in the Cason J. Callaway Memorial Forest runs along the road between the Callaway home and Blue Springs. It is called the Callaway Car Wash, because Miss Virginia used to drive through it to rinse the dust off of her car after a day in the forest.*

On to the Future

What do the years ahead hold for Callaway Gardens? One thing is certain: Thanks to an extremely generous donation by Ely Reeves Callaway Jr., founder of Callaway Golf Company, there is going to be a new, even more spectacular azalea garden.

The garden's new name will be The Callaway Brothers Azalea Bowl, named in loving memory of the deep, abiding personal ties and close professional relationship that existed between Mr. Cason's father, Fuller Earle Callaway Sr., and Fuller's half brother, Ely Reeves Callaway Sr. (Ely Jr.'s father). The fact of the matter is, if it weren't for the extraordinarily successful business endeavors of these two brothers, and the resulting fortune that was passed on to the next generation, Callaway Gardens would never have come into being. The founder and major driving force behind these enterprises, which include such companies as the Callaway Department Store, various Callaway banks, and the Callaway Textile Mills, was Fuller Sr. Once established, Fuller turned many of the day-to-day operations of these businesses over to the younger Ely Sr.

This bumblebee is taking nectar from a verbena (V. canadensis) *and, in turn, pollinating the flower.*

Azalea comes from the Greek word meaning "dry," which refers to the dry woods habitat where the shrub is often found in nature.

With the advent of The Callaway Brothers Azalea Bowl, even larger seas of azaleas will flourish, allowing ever growing numbers of visitors to enjoy their astonishing beauty.

It'll be tough to beat such a grand and ambitious undertaking as the azalea garden project, but Callaway Gardens is an ever-living, ever-renewing entity. Through careful steward-ship, it can be ours to enjoy for centuries.

Bo echoes this thought: "One of the things Dad said was that if you build a building, no matter how fine a building, it begins deteriorating and depreciating the next day. But if you build a garden and do it right, it begins appreciating the next day. There's no reason on earth why this garden can't be prettier in a hundred, two hundred, or a thousand years."

Other future plans hint at an increasing role for wildlife, especially in the as-yet-undeveloped wilderness areas, which constitute the largest part of the property. People eventually may be able to meet native fauna up close, just as they now meet native flora. Callaway Gardens will change, adapt, experiment. It must — for this garden, like any other, doesn't simply exist. It evolves.

"Grandfather never intended to finish this garden," concludes Bo Jr. "But neither does my father and neither do I. If we manage it well, this garden will continue to be a lifetime's work for the person who follows, and for generations to come."

With the completion of Callaway Gardens in the 1950s, Mr. Cason left a great legacy for the people of Georgia. Today, visitors from across the country and around the globe enjoy its simple, peaceful beauty and the quiet solitude of its gardens and trails. Future generations will continue to reap the benefits of Mr. Cason's prescient vision.

Callaway Gardens Bloom Calendar

Each season brings the expected joys of bloom and harvest — and each season enjoys its own internal calendar. What flowers in May nine years out of ten, may this year bloom in June. One autumn an early frost, one spring a late snow — each year's weather keeps the bloom predictors busy. The following bloom calendar shows what Callaway Gardens horticulturists predict for a typical year at the Gardens.

The blossoms of winter-blooming camellias (C. japonica) *stand out in a rare January snow at Callaway Gardens.*

JANUARY

- White-flowered paper bush (*Edgeworthia papyrifera*) and yellow-blooming Oregon grape holly (*Mahonia aquifolium*) send out their sturdy flowers along the pathways of the Holly Trail.
- Along the Holly Trail, fragrant winter jasmine (*Jasminum nudiflorum*) and winter honeysuckle (*Lonicera fragrantissima*) perfume the January air.
- Wander along the Holly Trail to discover unusual yellow-berried Chinese holly (*Ilex cornuta* 'D'or') among the red-berried evergreen hollies.

FEBRUARY

- Thousands of delicate yellow and orange witch hazel (*Hamamelis* spp.) blossoms seem to hover on their bare stems in bright contrast to the dark green hollies in Meadowlark Gardens.
- Nandina (*N. domestica*) berries hang in heavy clusters among shiny dark green and bronze leaves. Look for the unusual white form at the Day Butterfly Center's entrance drive.
- Early daffodils (*Narcissus* spp.), crocuses (*Crocus* spp.), and snowdrops (*Galanthus nivalis*) peek through evergreen ground covers and beds of brightly colored pansies (*Viola* x *wittrockiana*).
- Lenten roses (*Helleborus orientalis*) send out cream, lavender, and rosy flowers in shady areas throughout the Gardens.

MARCH

- Lavender redbud (*Cercis canadensis*), white magnolia (*Magnolia* spp.), and red buckeye (*Aesculus pavia*) trees bloom throughout the trails and along the drive.
- Daffodils (*Narcissus* spp.), tulips (*Tulipa* spp.), hyacinths (*H. orientalis*), and scillas (*Scilla* spp.) send their bright blooms up through beds of multicolored pansies (*Viola* x *wittrockiana*).
- Camellias (*C. japonica*), pieris (*P. japonica*), and forsythia (*Forsythia* x *intermedia*) shrubs color the trails and borders with red, pink, white, and yellow blossoms.
- Bright yellow Carolina jessamine (*Gelsemium sempervirens*) and muted red trumpet honeysuckle (*Lonicera sempervirens*) clamber over trellises and climb to the treetops along the trails.

APRIL

- Elegant fringe (*Chionanthus virginicus*) trees, native dogwoods (*Cornus florida*), and 'Callaway' crabapples (*Malus* 'Callaway') bloom white throughout the woods and in borders.
- The white, yellow, and pink blossoms of native azaleas (*Rhododendron* spp.) seem to float on their airy shrubs along the Scenic Drive.
- Brilliant pink, coral, red, and white cultivated azaleas (*Rhododendron* spp.) cover the azalea garden hillsides in the spring.
- The lacy white flowers of viburnum (*Viburnum* spp.), fothergilla (*Fothergilla* spp.), and spirea (*Spirea* spp.) shrubs appear along the drives and around Gardens structures.
- Foamflower (*Tiarella cordifolia*), rain lilies (*Zephyranthes atamasco*), firepink (*Silene virginica*), trillium (*Trillium* spp.), and columbine (*Aquilegia canadensis*) are some of the spring ephemerals — wildflowers that produce a brief but spectacular bloom — on the Wildflower Trail.
- Poppies (*Papaver* spp.), peonies (*Paeonia* spp.), late daffodils (*Narcissus* spp.), phlox (*Phlox* spp.), and snapdragons (*Antirrhinum majus*) fill the flower garden in spring.

MAY

- Mountain laurel (*Kalmia latifolia*) shrubs bloom in fist-sized clusters of pink and white along the Scenic Drive and Wildflower Trail.
- Pink evening primrose (*Oenothera speciosa*), lavender verbena (*Verbena canadensis*), and white false indigo (*Baptisia alba*) cover the sunny Wildflower Meadow with color.
- Evergreen rhododendrons (*Rhododendron* spp.) produce immense clusters of lavender, pink, or white flowers in the dappled sunlight along the Rhododendron Trail.
- Dianthus (*Dianthus* spp.), snapdragons (*Antirrhinum majus*), poppies (*Papaver* spp.), hollyhocks (*Alcea rosea*), and foxgloves (*Digitalis purpurea*) fill the flower borders with late spring color.
- The long, white bloom spikes of Virginia sweetspire (*Itea virginica*) shoot out of borders and woodland settings along the Scenic Drive.

Colorful flowers fill the borders at the Sibley Center during the fall months.

JUNE

- Native oakleaf hydrangeas (*H. quercifolia*) produce huge clusters of white flowers along the Scenic Drive.
- Pink-flowering Georgia fever (*Pinckneya pubens*) tree blooms profusely at the edges of the lakes. It is often difficult to spot, as it grows in islolated areas.
- Huge fragrant blossoms appear on the southern, big-leaf, and sweet bay magnolias (*M. grandiflora*, *M. macrophylla*, and *M. virginiana*).
- Sunny flower borders are filled with the bright rainbow colors of zinnias (*Z. elegans*), cosmos (*C. bipinnatus*), marigolds (*Tagetes* spp.), salvias (*Salvia* spp.), and sunflowers (*Helianthus* spp.).
- Southern blueberries (*Vaccinium ashei*) supply a bountiful harvest for gardeners and songbirds in Mr. Cason's Vegetable Garden.
- Dwarf clethra (*C. alnifolia* 'Hummingbird') is famous for its panicles of white flowers on the shores of Hummingbird Lake.

JULY

- Basil (*Ocimum basilium*), lemon verbena (*Aloysia triphylla*), and rosemary (*Rosmarinus officinalis*) fill the air with fragrance on hot summer nights in the Herb Garden at Mr. Cason's Vegetable Garden.
- Shady borders at the Sibley Center are packed with impatiens (I. *wallerana*), begonias (*Begonias* spp.), and caladiums (*Caladium* x *hortulanum*) at their peak.
- Plumleaf azalea (*Rhododendron prunifolium*), Callaway Gardens' signature plant, blooms bright red alongside the intensely fragrant white sweet azalea (*R. arborescens*) along Mountain Creek Trail and the Scenic Drive.
- Sourwood (*Oxydendron arboreum*) trees and bottlebrush buckeye (*Aesculus parviflora*) come into full bloom along the Scenic Drive.
- The bowed heads of the yellow and red flowers of pitcher plants (*Sarracenia* spp.) bloom in the bog garden on the Wildflower Trail.

AUGUST

- Crape myrtle (*Lagerstroemia indica*) trees are covered in pink blossoms along the Robin Lake Beach Dam.
- Spider lilies (*Lycoris radiata*) appear in red masses along the Holly Trail.
- The fragrant white flowers of the moonflower vine (*Ipomoea alba*) come into full bloom at Mr. Cason's Vegetable Garden.
- Water lilies (*Nelumbo lutea*) float on the surface of pools at the Sibley Center.

Blueberry bushes are covered with netting to protect the berries from mockingbirds.

SEPTEMBER

- Black and bronze muscadine grapes (*Vitis rotundifolia*), sweet potatoes (*Ipomea batatas*), and peanuts (*Arachis hypogaea*) reach harvest size at Mr. Cason's Vegetable Garden.
- Lantana (*L. camara*), cosmos (*Cosmos* spp.), and pineapple sage (*Salvia elegans*) bloom in bright reds and yellows, attracting migrating butterflies to flower borders throughout the Gardens.
- Clusters of bright purple or white berries ripen on the stems of American beautyberry (*Callicarpa americana*) along the Scenic Drive.

OCTOBER

- The Gardens glow with the bright harvest colors of chrysanthemums (*Chrysanthemum* x *morifolium*), fall-blooming salvia (*Salvia* spp.), and asters (*Aster* spp.).
- Huge Asian persimmons (*Diospyros kaki*) drag down the branches with their weight and tempt visitors at Mr. Cason's Vegetable Garden. Fall foliage color abounds in the woodlands throughout the Gardens: red, yellow, orange, and maroon seem to glow from the branches of sourwood (*Oxydendron arboreum*), maple (*Acer* spp.), oak (*Quercus* spp.), hickory (*Carya* spp.), and evergreen trees.
- The swamp sunflower (*Helianthus angustifolius*) sends up its brilliant golden blossoms to a towering 12 feet.

NOVEMBER

- Cascade chrysanthemums (*Chrysanthemum* spp.) seem to tumble over baskets and supports with their bright tapestries of color, which are the result of months of "training."
- The heady scent of tea olive (*Osmanthus* spp.) blossoms at the Sibley Center perfume the air whenever sunlight warms the tiny white flowers.
- The evergreen leaves of 'Callaway' wild ginger (*Hexastylis shuttle-worthii* 'Callaway') blanket the forest floor in tiny carpets along the Wildflower Trail.
- The soft plumes of ornamental grasses wave in the late fall breezes, adding motion to the borders at the Sibley Center.

DECEMBER

- Poinsettias (*Eurphorbia pulcherrima*) fill the Sibley Center for the holiday season. They are not actually flowers — the red, white, and pink "petals" are called bracts.
- Bright red and yellow berries cover the bare stems of deciduous hollies (*Ilex* spp.) along the Holly Trail.
- Cinnamon-colored crape myrtle (*Lagerstroemia indica*) bark and handsomely peeling paperbark maple (*Acer griseum*) and river birch (*Betula nigra*) create a lovely dark backdrop for the evergreens in the winter forest.
- The evergreen fronds of native Christmas fern (*Polystichum acros-tichoides*) appear in thick dark clumps among the fallen leaves of mixed hardwoods throughout the Gardens.

When Mountain Creek was first contained by this dam, 1,728,000 gallons of water per day poured into the reservoir that was to become Mountain Creek Lake. Even at this rate, it took a full year to fill the mammoth 175-acre lake.

Callaway Gardens Nature Notes

JANUARY
· Look for wintering ducks, like buffleheads, on the lakes.
· Flocks of robins and cedar waxwings gobble up every holly berry in sight.

FEBRUARY
· Bluebirds begin to scout for nesting locations.
· Spring peepers begin to call at night.
· Purple martins arrive from their winter homes in South America.
· Watch for a mourning cloak butterfly in flight on a sunny day.

MARCH
· Listen to the cheery music of songbirds (cardinals, chickadees, flickers, Carolina wrens) as they begin the nesting season.

APRIL
· Ruby-throated hummingbirds arrive from their overwintering grounds in Mexico and Central America. Watch for them nectaring on azaleas.

MAY
· Songbirds (cardinals, robins, titmice, woodpeckers) are busy feeding their young.

JUNE
· Fireflies light up summer evenings.
· Female water turtles wander across dry land searching for places to lay their eggs.

JULY
· Tiger swallowtail butterflies nectar on plumleaf azaleas.
· Bullfrogs bellow from the lakes at night.
· Colorful dragonflies dart through the air near the lakes.

AUGUST
· Purple martins depart for their wintering grounds in South America.

SEPTEMBER
· Watch kingfishers dive for fish in the lakes.

OCTOBER
· Monarch butterflies migrate through this area on their way to Mexico.
· Cloudless sulphur butterflies are commonly seen nectaring on fall-blooming flowers.

NOVEMBER
· Chipmunks and gray squirrels are busy eating the fall bounty of acorns.

DECEMBER
· Look for woodpeckers, titmice, chickadees, cardinals, and many other species of birds visiting the birdfeeders located throughout the Gardens.

This male cardinal brightens the forest in winter with his brilliant plumage.

Garden mums (Chrysanthemum *x* morifolium *'Lynn')* *are a traditional autumn favorite at Callaway Gardens.*

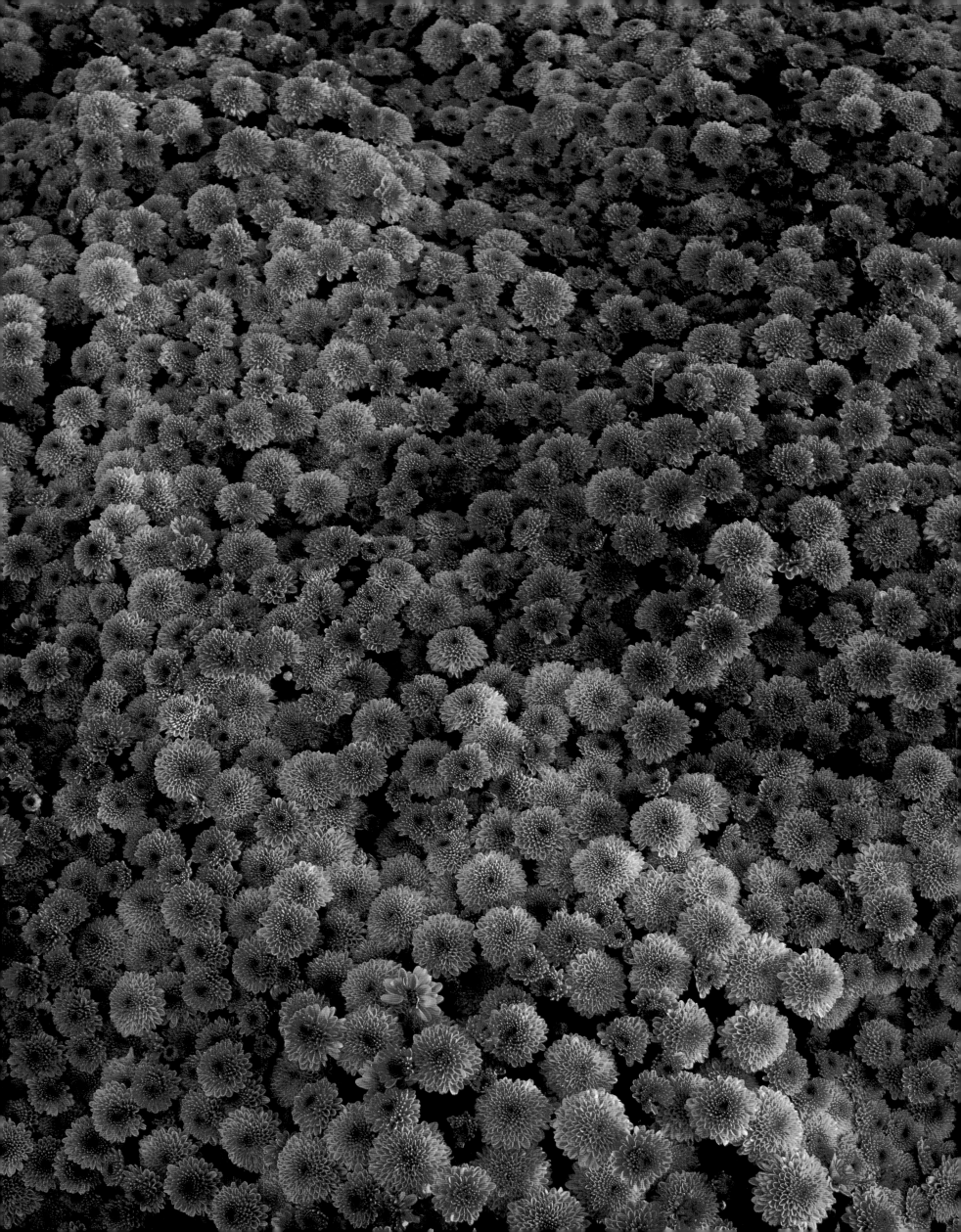

Index

Acknowledgments

Callaway Gardens and Callaway Editions would like to extend a warm and gracious thank you to the many people who have been involved in the creation of *Callaway Gardens: Legacy of a Dream*. It is a book worthy of the hard work and dedication that made it possible.

The Piedmont azalea (Rhododendron canescens) is the most abundant of all native azalea species of the South. The intensely fragrant flowers bloom in late March and early April.

Photograph, page 2: *One of Miss Virginia's favorite plants was mountain laurel* (Kalmia latifolia), *which makes a lovely canopy over the road between the Callaway family home and Blue Springs.*

The map that appears on pages 6–7 was illustrated by Lina Chesak.

Distributed by Longstreet Press.

ISBN 0-935112-25-1

Library of Congress Catalog Card Number 96-75430

First Edition

10 9 8 7 6 5 4 3 2 1

Printed by Palace Press International in Hong Kong.

This book was produced by Callaway Editions, Inc.

Nicholas Callaway, Editorial Director and Publisher
Andrea Danese, Editor
Toshiya Masuda, Designer
True Sims, Production Director
Paula Litzky, Associate Publisher
David Carriere, Publicity Director
Nancy Kenney, Contracts Manager
Kim Cheney, Proofreader

Monica Moran, Assistant to Nicholas Callaway
Sophia Seidner, Assistant to Paula Litzky
Jessica Allan, Assistant to True Sims
Christina Kulukundis, Assistant to Editors
Ivan Wong Jr., Jennifer Wagner, Sang-Joon Kang, John McCormick,
and José Rodríguez, Production Associates

Vicki Vessels Sumner, Creative Services Manager at Callaway Gardens, assisted Callaway Editions in all aspects of the editorial development of this project.

The text typeface is Minion by Adobe and Meyer Inscription, which was translated by Richard Beatty. Meyer Inscription is an Art Deco translation of Caslon. Mr. Beatty found this version on a 1928 tombstone in Cedar Hill Cemetery in Middle Hope, New York.

This book was printed and bound by Palace Press International, Hong Kong, under the supervision of Raoul Goff.

Fantasy In Lights ®

Callaway Gardens in Pine Mountain, Georgia (75 miles southwest of Atlanta), is a 14,000-acre Mobil four-star resort that includes a horticultural center, butterfly center, 63 holes of golf, 17 tennis courts, racquetball courts, nature trails, boating, fishing, fly-fishing, biking, and more. Callaway Gardens has a variety of accommodations (inn, cottages, and villas), real estate opportunities, seven restaurants, approximately 40,000 square feet of meeting and convention space, and many gift shops.

Annual special events include the Callaway School of Needlearts and the Southern Gardening Symposium, which take place every January. In springtime, gorgeous floral displays are highlighted during Spring Celebration, which includes a plant fair, an art show and sale, performing arts throughout the Gardens, family activities, and more. Memorial Day features international competition at the Masters Water Ski Tournament.

Summers at the Gardens are filled with family vacationers from across the country enjoying a week of Summer Family Adventure with age-appropriate day-camp activities and night-time family fun. The Florida State University "Flying High" Circus entertains daily (except Wednesdays) at Robin Lake Beach.

During the autumn months, some of the best golfers in the world come to Callaway Gardens for the PGA Tour® Buick Challenge. Autumn Adventure offers family activities throughout the Gardens. The Steeplechase at Callaway Gardens is the final U.S. leg of the prestigious Sport of Kings Challenge and features a day of races, music, art, and picnicking.

November and December light up with the nationally acclaimed Fantasy In Lights® Christmas light show featuring larger-than-life holiday displays throughout the Gardens. Environmental education workshops are available throughout the year.

Callaway Gardens

Pine Mountain, Georgia
1-800-CALLAWAY (225-5292)
www.callawaygardens.com